From Then and Now

Enya Cea-Lavin

BookLeaf Publishing

India | USA | UK

Presentation by *BookLeaf Publishing*

Web: www.bookleafpub.com

E-mail: info@bookleafpub.com

ISBN: 9789363309166

First edition 2024

Letter From Younger Me;
Brighter Path

I hope we take the brighter path
the one full of all the laughs.

We stick by those who love us most,
and stay away from those who don't.

Promise me to choose the brighter path
the one with the people who make you laugh

The Work of Art I am

Placed on a pedestal like a work of art.
Praised like a work of art.

Left on a shelf like a work of art.
Forgotten, broken and used by you.

Repainted over,
becoming a new canvas for you.

Tossed Aside

There for your conveniency,
when no one can.
I am left to wonder who I am,
waiting until you call me up.

I use the time that you toss me aside for.
Creating a better version,
A version you know longer will love or know.

Refusal To Love

Refused to love and refused to stay.
The one I thought wouldn't get away.
You chose to fight, making me think I wasn't
okay.

Feeling like the issue,
I raced to fix who I was.
Hoping to continue,
I revert the refusal to stay.

Haunted House

I shiver thinking of what we once were.
The terror and horror you brought to me,
the pain and distraught was stuck there,
like leaving a haunted house

You took who I was and turned her on her side,
tearing apart the good in me.

Put me through a haunted house and threw me
out.
Leaving me to rebuild, recreating Frankenstein.

Now Strangers

We laughed and danced, didn't think to fret
Lost track of time since the moment we met.

Lucky to get my hand on you,
get to be a part of you.

Now when I walk by,
I don't even know you.

I'm stuck strangled over now being strangers.

Grudge

My love for you was anger.

A one-sided grudge.

A way to turn from you,
to fuel my paint into you.

My love for you.
A grudge held against myself.

What's for Breakfast

how much do you really know about me
do you know how I like my morning coffee
or what I like for breakfast

I know how you like yours
a black coffee paired with a runny egg

even though it's not my favorite
I made it simpler for you to remember
as I say that's how i like mine too

Remember to Love You

I have to remind myself that you want me,
you beg for me as I push and turn away.

We've made mistakes
Yours unintended to hurt.
While, I use them to resist you.

I can't remember why you love me,
why you choose to stick by me.

Campus Lovers

Passing by you,
say hi to those who may know you.

Met first at a party,
the start of our true love story.

Now I awake,
from dreaming of you
to waking next to you.

Like the Ocean

Feeling the waves crash, and the sea part.
I stand, engulfed by the ocean in your eyes.

Getting swept into shore, lost through land.
Searching through, left at sea in your eyes.

My baby

They used to be cheesy
now I run around screaming them, thinking of
you.
I awake waiting for the time I get to call you
baby.

Thinking of new names that suit you,
maybe I relate it to a fruit, or a cute animal
maybe i'll just stick to baby.

Impact

You bring her out that child within.

The one that giggles, making everyone turn their head.
The one unafraid to make noise and be who she is.

She sits swinging her feet, unafraid of the space she takes.

That child within, happy to be brought out.

Used Book

to be loved like a used book
my reader soaking in every word
within the torn pages and molded spine
your love, like the passion of rereading my
favorites

where what once was torn
you hold the cover together
starting to highlight the best parts, analyzing the
difficulty,

looking past the dishevel
not being used once again
but being loved as a well used book

Me + You

Tell me why you want me,
why you chose to stand by me.

In your hands you hold me,
console me.

You whisper in my ear,
saying how much you love the way I love you.
Whispering to me about the best way to treat
you.

In this moment I learn,
why you want me and why I need you.

I Vow To You

I know I just met you
but I vow to never break you

In the palm of my hands,
I hope to hold your heart,
gentle and soft.

I vow to study you
like a work of art.

True Love Story

I see us,

I see us loving and laughing.
Remembering the jokes we made at twenty,
and singing a lovely jazz so gently.

I dream to be the one to hold you,
the one to wake you and worry.
One day I know I'll be your true love story.

A Promise to Younger Me

I promised to take the brighter path

I sit back as I laugh,
surrounded by those who love,
and away from those we shove.

I look around as I realize,
I took the brighter path.
The one full of those who make me laugh.

www.ingramcontent.com/pod-product-compliance
Lightning Source LLC
La Vergne TN
LVHW050312200726
843509LV00015B/3290